¡VIVA LOS SUEÑOS!

¡Viva los Sueños!

Sergio Serna

Joker &
the Queen
PUBLISHING

CONTENTS

Dedication viii

My Favorite Quote ix

- Photo Insert 1

- Sylvia Mendez Stood Up for School 2

- Photo Insert 3

- José Hernández & Ellen Ochoa: Space for All of Us 4

- Photo Insert 5

- Desi Arnaz Made America Laugh... Again and Again! 6

- Photo Insert 7

- Tom Flores Led His Team to Victory 8

- Photo Insert 9

- George and Mayan Lopez Shared the Laughs 10

- Photo Insert 11

- Laurie Hernández Danced Through the Air 12

- Photo Insert 13

- Elena Medo Helped Make Shots Hurt Less 14

– Photo Insert 15

– Guillermo González Camarena Brought Color to TV 16

– Photo Insert 17

– Lin-Manuel Miranda Let His Words Sing 18

– Photo Insert 19

– Rey Mysterio Showed What a Real Hero Looks Like 20

– Photo Insert 21

– A Special Message Just for You 22

About the Author 23

Published by Joker & the Queen Publishing

ISBN: 979-8-9992221-2-1

Printed in the United States of America

This book is a work of nonfiction. All stories are based on real individuals and real events. Some quotes have been simplified or paraphrased to suit young readers. This book is not authorized, endorsed, or sponsored by any individuals or organizations mentioned herein. It is intended solely as an educational and inspirational tribute.

Illustrations generated using AI technology under the creative direction of Sergio Serna

Book design by: Sergio Serna

First Edition

10 9 8 7 6 5 4 3 2 1

To all the dreamers—
To everyone who feels deep down that they're meant for greatness,
The golden ring is yours for the taking.
To every kid just starting their school journey,
And to every student past, present, and future
Who's ever walked through Ms. Castro's Kindergarten class...
This one's for you.

MY FAVORITE QUOTE

Be not afraid of greatness.
Some are born great,
some achieve greatness,
and some have greatness thrust upon them.
— William Shakespeare
   (The author's favorite quote)

SYLVIA MENDEZ STOOD UP FOR SCHOOL

S ylvia loved to learn.
She wore her best dress, tied her shoes tight,
and held her mommy's hand.
   But when she got to the big school near her house,
the lady said,
"No. You can't come in. This school is only for white children."
   Sylvia didn't understand.
She lived right down the street.
She spoke English.
She was ready to learn.
   But the sign on the school said "No Mexicans."
That made Sylvia sad. And mad.
   So her family went to court.
They said, "Sylvia belongs in that school."
   The fight was long.
It took many days.
But one day, the judge said,
"Yes. Sylvia can go. And so can all the other kids, too."
   Sylvia smiled.
She walked into school with her head held high.
She made space for kids like Ruby Bridges
to walk through more doors later on.
   **What would you do if someone told you "no" when you knew it
should be "yes"?**

JOSÉ HERNÁNDEZ & ELLEN OCHOA: SPACE FOR ALL OF US

José dreamed of space while picking strawberries.
 Ellen dreamed of space while reading books.
They came from different places—
but they looked up at the same stars.
    They studied.
They worked hard.
They never gave up.
    José flew to space.
Ellen flew to space.
And both of them showed the world
that Latino kids can reach the stars too.
    Now when a child looks up at the sky and says,
"Could I go there someday?"
the answer is simple:
    Yes.
There is space for all of us—
in science, in school, in dreams,
and among the stars.
    What do you dream about doing one day?

DESI ARNAZ MADE AMERICA LAUGH... AGAIN AND AGAIN!

Desi loved to perform.
He played the drums.
He danced and sang.
He made people laugh.
    He came from Cuba with big dreams.
And he didn't stop chasing them.
    Desi starred on a show called *I Love Lucy*
with his real-life wife, Lucy.
He was funny, kind, and always full of energy.
    But Desi didn't just act—
he helped make the show behind the scenes too.
    He had a big idea:
"What if we film the show,
so people can watch it again later?"
    That idea became the rerun!
    Because of Desi,
people could laugh at their favorite shows again and again.
Even when the actors weren't on stage anymore.
    Desi changed how TV worked—
and he made sure Latino kids could dream big on screen and behind the camera
too.
    What kind of show would you make if you could put one on TV?

TOM FLORES LED HIS TEAM TO VICTORY

Tom loved football.
He threw the ball far.
He called plays.
He dreamed of being a star.
    But when Tom was young,
there weren't many players like him in the game.
And there were *no* Latino head coaches.
    Tom didn't give up.
He became a quarterback.
Then he became a coach.
He worked hard and believed in his team.
    One day, Tom's team won the biggest game of all—
the Super Bowl!
And then... they won it again.
    Tom made history.
The first Latino head coach to win it all.
Twice!
    Because Tom showed what leadership looks like,
kids everywhere could say,
"I can do that too."
    What kind of team would you want to lead?

GEORGE AND MAYAN LOPEZ SHARED THE LAUGHS

George loved to make people laugh.
He told jokes about growing up Latino,
about his big family,
and about real life.
   Some people said,
"Those stories aren't for TV."
But George said,
"Yes they are—because they're real."
   George made a show with a Latino family.
It was the first time many kids
saw someone like them on TV.
   Years later,
his daughter Mayan had stories to tell too.
Funny ones. Honest ones.
Ones that were all her own.
   So she teamed up with her dad
to make a brand-new show—
one that shows how families can be silly, real,
and full of love.
   Because George and Mayan shared their voices,
now more kids can laugh,
see their own families on screen,
and dream up stories of their own.
   What story would you tell about your family?

LAURIE HERNÁNDEZ DANCED THROUGH THE AIR

Laurie loved to move.
She twirled. She flipped. She flew.
She smiled big every time she landed.
    She trained for hours.
She practiced her balance,
her jumps,
and her strength.
    Laurie became a gymnast—
a really good one.
And then...
an Olympic one.
    At the Olympics, Laurie wowed the world.
She leaped and danced with joy.
She won a gold medal
and a silver one too!
    People called her "the human emoji"
because she always smiled.
    Laurie showed that being strong
and being yourself
can go hand in hand.
    Because Laurie believed in her magic,
kids everywhere could say,
"I can shine like that too."
    What makes you feel strong and happy?

ELENA MEDO HELPED MAKE SHOTS HURT LESS

Elena wanted to help people.
She saw kids who were scared of shots.
She saw grown-ups who didn't have easy ways to get medicine.
So she started thinking...
What if we could give medicine *without* a needle?
Elena worked hard.
She studied science.
She asked big questions.
And she created a new way to give medicine
that used a soft spray instead of a sharp poke.
It helped kids feel brave.
It helped doctors and nurses all over the world.
Because Elena cared and kept asking "What if?",
she made a big difference in a small, gentle way.
Now more people can get the help they need—
without fear.

What problem would you like to solve to help people?

GUILLERMO GONZÁLEZ CAMARENA BROUGHT COLOR TO TV

Guillermo loved to build things.
When he was a little boy in Mexico,
he took apart radios and made new inventions.
He even built his own TV camera—at just 12 years old!
   But one day, he had a big idea:
"What if TV wasn't just black and white?
What if we could see it... in color?"
   Guillermo worked and worked.
He tested wires and lights and screens.
And guess what?
   He invented a color TV system
that helped bring color to homes all around the world!
   Because Guillermo used his imagination,
the world got a little brighter.
And kids like you could dream in every color too.
   If you could invent something, what would it do?

LIN-MANUEL MIRANDA LET HIS WORDS SING

Lin loved music.
He loved stories.
He loved the way words could dance.
    As a kid, he wrote songs in his room.
He told stories about his family,
his home,
and his dreams.
    One day, he made a show called *Hamilton*.
It mixed hip-hop, history, and heart.
And it made people feel something *new*.
    Then he made *In the Heights*,
a story about his neighborhood—
full of music, love, and Latino pride.
    Lin's words were big, bold, and beautiful.
They told the world,
"We belong in the spotlight too."
    Because Lin-Manuel shared his voice,
He opened the stage for so many more to follow.
    If you could write a song, what would it be about?

REY MYSTERIO SHOWED WHAT A REAL HERO LOOKS LIKE

Rey wasn't the biggest.
He wasn't the tallest.
But when he flew through the air in his mask,
everyone stopped and watched.

Rey came from a long line of luchadores—
wrestlers who told stories with their moves,
their colors,
and their hearts.

People said he was too small.
They said he couldn't do it.

But Rey didn't listen.
He trained.
He fought.
He believed.

He became a champion.
A legend.
A hero to millions.

Because Rey wore his culture with pride
and flew higher than anyone thought possible,
kids everywhere knew—

You don't have to fit the mold to be mighty.
What makes *you* feel powerful?

Don't let anyone tell you
the sky is the limit,
when there are
footprints on the moon.

A SPECIAL MESSAGE JUST FOR YOU

You've met so many amazing people in this book.
They were dreamers, doers, helpers, and leaders.
And guess what? So are you.

You belong in every classroom.
On every team.
In every story.
In every dream.

Some people might say,
"You can't do that,"
or "That's not for someone like you."

But they're wrong.

Because you are smart.
You are strong.
You are full of ideas and heart.

And don't let anyone tell you the sky's the limit—
when there are footprints on the moon.

So dream big.
Ask questions.
Speak up.
Shine bright.

The world needs your voice.

The world needs *you.*

Sergio Serna is a proud Latino writer, father, and storyteller. He believes that every child deserves to see themselves as heroes, dreamers, and leaders. Inspired by his own family, community, and culture, Sergio created ¡*Viva los Sueños!* to remind young readers that their voice matters—and that greatness can come from anywhere.

He is also the author of *One Nation: The Untold Story of Raider Nation*, a book about the fans who made a football team into a family.

He hopes this book helps you dream big, stay proud of who you are, and never stop believing in what's possible.

This is only the beginning.